Wonders
of Karnak

Karnak: the Sacred Lake

Wonders *of* Karnak

The Sound and Light of Thebes

Introduced by
Zahi Hawass

Misr Company for Sound, Light, & Cinema—Cairo
Distributed by the American University in Cairo Press

Copyright © 2009 by
Misr Company for Sound, Light, & Cinema
Abu-l-Hol Square, Nazlet al-Semman, Pyramids, Giza
www.soundandlight.com.eg

Produced and distributed by the American University in Cairo Press
113 Sharia Kasr el Aini, Cairo, Egypt
420 Fifth Avenue, New York, NY 10018
www.aucpress.com

Photographs by Emad Allam, pages: cover, ii, vi, 4, 6, 10, 12–13, 16, 24–43, 47, 76, 89
Photographs by Sandro Vannini (© Sandro Vannini/SCA Archive), pages: 44–46, 48–75

Dar el Kutub No. 13814/09
ISBN 978 977 177 342 9

Dar el Kutub Cataloging-in-Publication Data

Hawass, Zahi
        Wonders of Karnak: The Sound and Light of Thebes / Introduced by Zahi
    Hawass.—Cairo: Misr Company for Sound, Light, & Cinema, 2009
            p.   cm.
            ISBN 978 977 177 342 9
            1. Theater—sound effects   2. Temples—Egypt
            I. Hawass, Zahi (intro)

1 2 3 4 5 6 7 8   14 13 12 11 10 09

Designed by Sally Boylan
Printed in Egypt

Contents

Acknowledgments

The first edition of this book appeared in 1975 to celebrate the inauguration of the Sound and Light show at Luxor's Karnak Temple. The Karnak Temple, which was opened on December 19, 1972, was the third in a series of venues chosen for the Sound and Light projects in Egypt, following programs running at the Pyramids and Sphinx in Giza, and the Citadel in Cairo.

Over the years, the Sound and Light show has seen substantial technological development in tools, equipment, and artistic effects, most recently in 1994 and 2008. For the thirty-sixth anniversary of the show, Misr Company for Sound, Light, & Cinema carried out a comprehensive overhaul of the equipment, sound and light effects, electronic controls, and computer systems. State-of-the-art technology has been used to create an all-new advanced sound recording.

By chance the Karnak Temple was at the same time undergoing restoration. The forecourt of the temple, which extends to the bank of the River Nile, was renovated, as was the sacred avenue of sphinxes linking Karnak and Luxor temples.

We would like to thank Egyptian Minister of Culture Farouk Hosni for his valuable direction during the preparation of the development project and the preservation of the original multilingual recording.

Our deepest thanks also go to Dr. Zahi Hawass, secretary general of the Supreme Council of Antiquities, who revised and abridged the text and selected the images used in the show.

We also thank General Samir Farag, governor of Luxor, for his comprehensive initiative to develop Luxor city, the area surrounding Karnak temple in particular. His efforts have turned Luxor into one of the most beautiful ancient cities in the world, ultimately enhancing the value of the Sound and Light development project.

Our deep appreciation goes to the Cairo Opera House for their expert supervision of the musical recordings of the show and their gracious loan of their studios and music sets. This was the first time a Sound and Light show has been recorded at an Egyptian studio and by an Egyptian team.

We would also like to praise the sincere efforts of the workers at the Luxor antiquities sites, without whom the project could not have been carried out with such precision and beauty.

Finally, our thanks and appreciation to all those at Misr Company for Sound, Light & Cinema, including experts, consultants, engineers, technicians, and workers at both the engineering sector and onsite at Karnak, for their efforts over the course of the three-year duration of the project.

Eng. Essam Abdel Hadi
Chairman and Managing Director,
Misr Company for Sound, Light, & Cinema

The Karnak Sound and Light Show
Gaston Bonheur, script
Georges Delerue, musical score
Gaston Papeloux, scenario
Har Hollands and Kees Bos, artistic directors
Toon Thellier, technical director

Executive Engineers
Fawzi Ahmad Abd al-Hamid
Muhammad Raafat Abdalla Shaeer
Bushra Barsoum Abd al-Messeih
Kamal Rabie Yasin
Inji Ibrahim
Hani Fathi Abu al-Yazid
Reda Hasan Ahmad
Radi Masri Afandi

Executive Technicians
Abd al-Baset Muhammad Amin
Muhammad Kamal Ali Madani
Imam Saleh Abd al-Baset
Muhammad Khalafallah Ahmad
Ali Muhammad Salem
Ismail Muhammad Ismail

Cairo Opera House Team
Muhammad Hamdi, head of the Technical Musical Committee
Tareq Mahran, conductor
Nashaat Nasr al-Din, sound engineering director
Muhammad Ismail, sound engineer

Preface

Zahi Hawass

The temples of Karnak are the only monuments in the world that can tell us about the respective periods of ancient Egyptian history. On their walls are chronicled the lives of the great rulers who built the empire of the Golden Age. Among these kings is the great pharaoh Tuthmosis III who waged the battle of Megiddo, the first on record, and whose great scientists collected information and, also for the first time, drew the landscape of the east. From these inscriptions we have gleaned a wealth of information about religion and foreign relations in ancient Egypt, while ongoing archaeological excavations continue to yield wonderful new discoveries.

In 1903 a great cache of 17,000 objects, including beautiful statues, was found in the Hypostyle Hall. In the third pylon at Karnak the dismantled blocks of the Red Chapel of Hatshepsut were found; these have now been reconstructed in the Open-Air Museum at Karnak. One of the greatest moments for me was discovering, while working with the French–Egyptian team at Karnak in 2005, about five meters under the obelisk of Queen Hatshepsut, a double statue of Neferhotep dating to the Thirteenth Dynasty.

All of this magic and myth can be relived through the spectacle of the Sound and Light show—an experience one can never forget.

rnak: the Great
postyle Hall

Thebes and the Golden Age of the Pharaohs

Zahi Hawass

Since antiquity visitors have traveled to Egypt from all over the world to see and enjoy the wonders and blessings bestowed upon this land. They come to behold the sites of a great civilization that flourished when the world was still in its infancy. They come to see the vast artistic and architectural heritage that has immortalized the ancient Egyptian civilization—a heritage that has been an object of wonder for centuries. For decades we have attempted to uncover the glorious achievements of the past from these immortal ruins, the ruins which, until just years ago, were merely peaceful, still pictures suggestive of man's genius. Today, modern technology and scientific progress have made expression possible for that which was once silent and motionless.

It is the miracle of art and science in the twentieth century that creates the Sound and Light experience. The popularity of this modern artistic spectacle began to spread following its first exhibition at the Palace of Versailles in 1952. It then came to the banks of the Nile, first at the Giza Pyramids in 1961, where the Great Sphinx told us the secrets of its history and related examples, experiences, and sensations from the past. In

7

1962 the Salah al-Din Citadel began to recount the history of an immortal, courageous city—the city of Cairo. The project, however, was discontinued and, since 1972, Karnak has revealed its secrets in one of the largest, most modern, and outstanding Sound and Light venues in the world. It chronicles the past of the ancient city of Thebes, introducing its monuments in a spectacular, artistic representation combining vivid pictures, a dramatic scenario, and expressive music. The experience enables one to witness the magic and mystery of Egypt's Golden Age: the New Kingdom.

The Sound and Light show invites you to visit the Karnak temples at night, witness the story of the pharaohs, sit by the sacred lake, and listen to the voices of the past. Sound, music, and lighting effects harmonize to present a panorama in which civilizations, dead for thousands of years, are vividly reborn. Heroes of antiquity arise, greater and more powerful than in life, while voices echoing from the past relate the dramas of history and reveal the secrets and philosophies of our immortal ancestors.

The Sound and Light experience offers unlimited educational and cultural value. It has aroused an interest in culture and the desire of thousands of visitors—from Egypt and abroad—to gain more knowledge; it has stimulated the love for all forms of art and a delight in history and the artifacts of the past. It is also an audio-visual educational tool presenting science, art, and culture in an appealing package, especially for young people.

Thanks to the show, daylight is no longer the only time when monuments can be viewed. The lighting effects on the historical monuments produce a unique experience that invokes the full powers of the spectator's imagination and weaves unforgettable memories. The glow of the moon was for a long time the only illumination allowing us to see monuments during the night. No doubt the sight was poetic and had a serene beauty, but the Sound and Light show made that which was once limited to a few nights every month possible every night of the year.

The experience is a wonderful way to end a day of exploration in Luxor. It is truly thrilling to walk through the vast temple complex at night, with dramatic illumination highlighting different elements of the monument, and a stirring narrative explaining the history of the temple while evoking images of the ancient past.

Now, let us explore the marvelous history and archaeology of the Karnak and Luxor temples, dive into the mysteries of the royal tombs in the Valley of the Kings, and investigate the concepts of paradise depicted on the walls of the Tombs of the Nobles and in the reliefs of the mortuary temples on the west bank.

Karnak

From the beginning of the New Kingdom, every king in ancient Egypt built temples, chapels, and statues which, when combined, created the complex now known as the Temple of Karnak. As a reward for their devotion, Amon, universal god and god of war, granted the New Kingdom pharaohs military victories. The New Kingdom saw the expansion of temples funded by tributes of gold awarded to the victorious pharaohs and dedicated to the god Amon. Ancient Egypt's vast richness has been demonstrated numerous times, such as on November 4, 1922, when Howard Carter found the tomb of Tutankhamon; all he could see was "Gold. . . . Everywhere the glint of gold." When Lord Carnarvon arrived in Luxor to visit the newly uncovered tomb, he asked Carter, "What do you see?" and Carter answered, "Wonderful things . . . wonderful things." Egypt was always rich with gold. The Turin Papyrus Map, now in the Turin Museum, indicates the location of gold mines in Nubia. Moreover, the abundance of gold in Egypt is reflected in a letter sent by the King of Mitanni to the Egyptian Pharaoh Amenhotep III: "Send me gold, because gold in your country is like dust."

The sacred land encompassing the temples of Karnak was used not only for Amon, also known as Amon-Re, but for other gods such as Ptah, god of artisans at Memphis; Khonsu, the son of Amon and Mut; and the Aten, the one god, among others.

The earliest building at the site dates to the Middle Kingdom, a beautiful limestone chapel built by Senwosret I and known as the "White Chapel." Amenhotep I was the first king of the New Kingdom to erect a

temple to Amon at Karnak, considered a sacred spot in the Middle Kingdom. Later, Tuthmosis I added to the construction by building the Fourth and Fifth Pylons. Queen Hatshepsut added two obelisks between these Fourth and Fifth Pylons. The northern one is still standing and measures 29.25 meters in height.

The great king Tuthmosis III built chapels in the court of Tuthmosis I and erected the Sixth and the Seventh Pylons. He also constructed two rooms for the Annals; the west room is marked by two columns of red granite, one symbolizing the north with a papyrus shape and the other symbolizing the south with a lotus flower. He then added a hall called the Akhmenu, or 'hall of festivals,' on the eastern end of the temple. The Third Pylon was built by the great king Amenhotep III.

The Temples of Karnak

The temples of Karnak are among the most impressive temples in Egypt, eliciting awe and wonder in the thousands who come to visit them because of their unique architectural components. Among the most popular sites are the Hypostyle Hall constructed during the reign of Seti I and the Annals' Room of Tuthmosis III. Scholars refer to this king as the "Napoleon of Ancient Egypt." When Tuthmosis III set out on his eastern campaigns to Syria and Palestine, he brought many countries under his control and created a considerable empire. Tuthmosis III waged military campaigns for two decades, including on the fortified town of Megiddo. The strategies put in place during the battle of Megiddo are still studied today in military colleges around the world.

These campaigns also enriched Egypt's own culture. The sons of leaders from distant lands were brought to Egypt during this period to study at the royal palace. Scientists who accompanied Tuthmosis III on his campaigns recorded properties of foreign plants and described them in the king's annals. Tuthmosis III also brought foreign birds back to Egypt; chickens were first introduced here during his reign.

The pharaoh's numerous military conquests meant that the great god Amon, known as the "hidden one" and for whom the main temple of

rnak: the Great
postyle Hall

Karnak was built, was worshiped all over the empire, his name being spoken by all. One can imagine the magical sight of Pharaoh Tuthmosis III returning victorious to Thebes, the capital of Egypt during its Golden Age, to bestow tribute upon the god Amon, who would be pleased by the king's advances into foreign lands.

The temple of Karnak was the domain of the god Amon; it was considered his 'house.' The temple of Luxor was also dedicated to a form of the god Amon. Other chapels and structures within the enclosures of these two temples were dedicated to Mut and Khonsu, the wife and son of the god Amon, to complete what is now called the Theban Triad. At each of these temples, the cult of the god was performed daily.

One of the most impressive journeys of the god Amon, however, occurred annually. It was known as the Beautiful Feast of Opet, in which the god's cult statue left the temple of Karnak to visit the Pharaoh at Luxor Temple

Karnak: the Sacred Lake

so that he might give him the powers of kingship as the living Horus falcon. This union symbolized fertility manifested in the annual Nile floods.

During the reign of Tuthmosis III this festival lasted eleven days. The statue of the god Amon was placed on the sacred bark, which was carried by priests and transported by land. The return leg of the journey from Luxor was made on water. The rituals associated with this festival celebrated the sacred marriage between Amon and Mut.

Akhenaten and the Sun God

One of the most defining moments in Egyptian history, and also in the history of the world, was when Amenhotep IV, son of Amenhotep III, took the throne and decreed that Egyptians were to abandon the worship of their gods, including the great god Amon-Re, and worship a single god, the "Aten," whose power was concentrated in the sun-disk. This king

changed his name to Akhenaten, and built a temple for his new god inside the precinct of Karnak, igniting a conflict between the priests of Amon and those of the Aten. Akhenaten decided to leave Karnak to Amon and his priests, and founded a new capital and place for the worship of the "one god"—the site of Tell al-Amarna in Middle Egypt. It was called Akhet-Aten, meaning "the Horizon of the Aten."

Akhenaten lived in Amarna with his beautiful wife, Nefertiti, and their six children. But Akhenaten's biggest mistake was in making the Aten inaccessible to common Egyptians. Being forced to worship the new god through the king meant that after his death they could no longer communicate with the sun-disk. Tutankhaten, a member of the royal family, was raised in Amarna and later became king, leaving the new capital after the death of Akhenaten, and returning to Thebes. Tutankhaten began his reign at the age of nine and changed his name to Tutankhamon. He re-established the political and religious power at Thebes, and re-instated the priests of Amon.

Over the years, structures were added to the temple of Karnak. These additions continued well into the Ptolemaic and Roman periods. Since then, the Karnak Temple has granted us many surprises. Who could forget the great discovery in 1902 of the Karnak cachet filled with about 17,000 objects, including over 150 statues?

The Luxor Temple is another important site built during Egypt's Golden Age. Its construction was begun during the reigns of Hatshepsut and Amenhotep III. The First Pylon, however, was erected under Ramesses II. Originally, two obelisks fronted the entrance to the temple. Today, one of them stands in Place de la Concorde in Paris along with two statues. The Luxor Temple's second hall is decorated with scenes from the Opet Feast and dates to the reign of Tutankhamon. Lastly, the unique hypostyle hall dates to the reign of Amenhotep III. Onsite within his mortuary temple are a great statue of the king as well as one of his wife, Queen Tiye. Over thirty statues of the lioness goddess Sekhmet were found along with Amenhotep III and Tiye's statues. Sekhmet was the goddess of war, but was also related to protective and healing aspects.

The West Bank

On the west bank, facing the temples of Karnak and Luxor, are great mortuary temples built to preserve the memory of pharaohs and gods, called "Temples of Millions of Years."

During the Old and Middle Kingdoms, mortuary temples were attached to the tomb of the king. During the New Kingdom, the Egyptians separated the temples from the tombs, and built them along the edge of the desert near the cultivated land, starting in the northeast and stretching to the southwest for a distance of seven and a half kilometers. The first New Kingdom mortuary temple was built by Amenhotep I, whose tomb has not yet been found. Archaeologists are still searching for it in the cliffs of Deir al-Bahari.

The temples on the West Bank were built for the worship of gods and kings. The temple of Nebhepetre Mentuhotep, first king of the Middle Kingdom's Eleventh Dynasty, is fronted by a causeway and statues of the ruler. In 1900, Howard Carter, the famous archaeologist, was riding along the processional causeway when his horse's leg stumbled into a hole. This hole turned out to be a shaft which led to a series of unfinished rooms within the mortuary temple. A beautiful statue of Mentuhotep II was found inside the shaft, and is now in the Egyptian Museum, Cairo. The shaft is known in Arabic as Bab al-Hosan, which means the 'door of the horse.' Scholars are still debating the design of Mentuhotep's temple, as to whether it was topped by a pyramid or by a simple square base.

To the north of Mentuhotep's temple, Queen Hatshepsut—who reigned during the New Kingdom's Eighteenth Dynasty—ordered her architect, Senenmut, to build her a temple. It took a total of fifteen years to complete. It is partly rock-cut and partly stone-built, erected on three terraces that included courts separated by colonnades linked through a series of ramps. On the west side of the open court are twenty-two pillars in two rows and a statue of the queen. The most important scenes are recorded in the lower colonnade, and show the transportation of two large obelisks from Aswan to the temple of Amon at Karnak. On the second terrace in the colonnade are scenes of the divine birth and coronation of Hatshepsut on the northern end, while on the southern end are the famous Punt expedition scenes.

Recent studies now suggest that Punt is located between Ethiopia and Sudan. The scenes of Punt are important because of their depiction of the exotic landscape of a foreign country, in addition to the representation of the arrival of the queen of Punt by donkey.

Although other queens had ruled as pharaoh during periods of unrest, Hatshepsut was the only woman to rule Egypt during its Golden Age, a time of prosperity and stability. For many years, scholars believed that Hatshepsut stole the throne from her stepson, Tuthmosis III, who later killed her and destroyed all her monuments. Her mummy was actually found in 1903 by Howard Carter in the tomb known as KV 60. KV 60 is located very close to KV 20, Hatshepsut's original tomb. When Carter opened it in 1903, he discovered one of the mummies lying in a coffin which was inscribed with the name "In," the second half of the name of Hatshepsut's wet-nurse, Sitre-In. In 1906, the British archaeologist Edward Ayrton re-excavated KV 60 and moved In's coffin and the mummy it contained to the Egyptian Museum in Cairo, where they lay in storage on the museum's third floor for many years. They were never studied, and no photographs of them existed. The second mummy in KV 60 was that of an obese, older woman. When Carter opened KV 60 in 1903, it lay on the tomb's floor without a coffin. At the time when In's coffin and its mummy were moved to Cairo, the obese mummy was left behind inside the tomb. As early as 1966, Elizabeth Thomas had suggested that this mummy, known as KV 60-A, might be that of Hatshepsut. It was only in 2007 that the Egyptian Mummy Project was able to confirm that KV 60-A was indeed Hatshepsut. The discovery of scenes in the Red Chapel at Karnak depicting the queen behind Tuthmosis III as king demonstrate that he did not murder her. It is now believed that the destruction of her monuments occurred at the end of Tuthmosis III's reign and at the start of his son's reign, Amenhotep II, by detractors who did not wish to see Hatshepsut rule as pharaoh.

In 1881, a great discovery occurred behind Hatshepsut's temple. This discovery involved a cache of mummies, now known as DB 320. The story began earlier, however, when a man named Ahmad Abd al-Rassul was leading a herd of goats and sheep. One animal escaped from the herd, and the man was forced to run after it. The goat stumbled and disappeared down a tomb shaft. When Abd al-Rassul entered the shaft, he saw treasures of gold and silver.

The Abd al-Rassul family entered the cache several times, and began to sell off some of the objects. Gaston Maspero, then the director of the Antiquities Service, spotted one of these objects for sale at the market. An investigation began, which led to the arrest and imprisonment of one member of the family. He was later released from jail and demanded from his family a greater share of the treasure to compensate for his suffering. The family began to fight until one member finally informed the police about the location of the cache. In 1881, about forty mummies were moved to the Bulaq museum in Cairo.

The third great temple located on the west bank is the temple of Amenhotep III, built during the Eighteenth Dynasty of the New Kingdom. Today, what remains aboveground are two colossal sandstone statues of Amenhotep III, known as the Colossi of Memnon, each measuring about eighteen meters in height, and weighing approximately 700 tons each.

In 27 BC an earthquake caused the upper part of the northern statue to collapse. Legend has it that from that moment onward the statue would produce a strange sound at dawn, like a voice on the wind. The Greeks called the statue Memnon, a hero of the Trojan war, later slain by Achilles. The Colossi of Memnon became famous over time, and tourists used to travel to Thebes in order to see them. The Emperor Hadrian and his wife came to visit them in 130 AD. During the reign of the Roman emperor Septimius Severus (193–211 AD), the northern colossus was restored, and the voice on the wind disappeared forever.

The Ramesseum is another great temple. It was built by Ramesses II in the Nineteenth Dynasty of the New Kingdom. The temple was called the Memnonium because of the colossal statue in the temple, similar to that of the Colossi of Memnon. The temple was begun in the second year of Ramesses II's reign and was completed some twenty years later. It is surrounded by a huge mud-brick wall, measuring about 270 meters in length. The First Pylon is about sixty-six meters wide, and is decorated with scenes of the battle of Kadesh, also depicted in the temples of Karnak, Luxor, Abydos, and Abu Simbel. The Ramesseum is one of the most remarkable temples on the west bank.

The other great temple is the temple of Ramesses III, known as Medinet Habu. It is the largest temple, measuring 150 meters in length. The depictions on its walls show the king smiting his enemies, including the Libyans and the Sea Peoples who attacked Egypt during the king's reign. The most interesting scenes in this temple are located on the back of the south tower of the First Pylon. Ramesses III, the last great warrior king, is shown hunting wild bulls, some of which already have arrows stuck in their bodies. We can clearly see the pain on their faces.

The Valley of the Queens

The Valley of the Queens was called the "beautiful place" by the ancient Egyptians, and was used as a burial place between the Nineteenth and Twentieth Dynasties. The valley contains about ninety tombs, but the most famous and beautiful of them is the one belonging to Queen Nefertari, wife of Ramesses II. The tomb has a sloping entrance that leads to the first hall, which contains scenes of Queen Nefertari worshiping the jackal god Anubis and others. There is also the famous scene of the queen with the goddess Isis. These scenes are astonishing for their fresh colors that look as if they were just recently painted. The different ways in which the queen is depicted, her various types of dress, and her relationship to Hathor, goddess of love and beauty in ancient Egypt, never fail to enthrall visitors to the tomb.

The Tombs of the Nobles

Approximately five hundred tombs of nobles have been discovered in Thebes. The areas containing these tombs are divided into small necropolises with modern names. The necropolis of Sheikh Abd al-Qurna was completely filled with tombs by the end of Tuthmosis IV's Eighteenth Dynasty reign, causing the high officials of Amenhotep III to look for a new location.

One of the most famous tombs in Sheikh Abd al-Qurna belongs to Rekhmire, who was the vizier of Tuthmosis III. His tomb is famous for a text that details the duties of the office of vizier. This text is located on the west wall of the first chamber. In fact, we call this chamber the hall of the vizier as his various duties are depicted, such as inspecting tribute. The main chapel shows various scenes, including well-known scenes of craftsmen.

Also located in Sheikh Abd al-Qurna is the tomb of Menna, which dates to the reign of Tuthmosis IV. Scenes in this tomb include ones of daily life, in which his family is listening to a man sitting and playing the flute.

The tomb of Nakht, also located in Sheikh Abd al-Qurna, has unique scenes of festivals. It is possible that it dates to the reign of Tuthmosis IV. In the tomb, scenes show guests sitting, while a blind man plays music. One of the most famous scenes in this tomb depicts the making of wine.

The tomb of Sennefer is also located in Sheikh Abd al-Qurna. Sennefer was an important official during the reign of Amenhotep II. His tomb is known as the "tomb of the vineyards," because of the grapes drawn on parts of the ceiling.

Deir al-Medina

The workmen who constructed the royal tombs in the Valley of the Kings lived at Deir al-Medina. This village was known as the "house of truth," and contains the ruins of approximately seventy houses. The workmen lived in this village from the reign of Tuthmosis I onward. The village is famed for its many important legal cases surrounding the lives of its occupants. Deir al-Medina has records of court cases, such as the following case between two women: In the early years of the reign of Ramesses II, the wife of a local official, named Irynofret, decided to purchase a slave girl worth around four deben and paid for her with a variety of commodities. But before she had time to make use of her new purchase, her neighbor, Bakmut, claimed that some of her property had been used to complete the purchase, and she, therefore, had claims on the hapless girl. Eventually, Bakmut took her claim to court, and both women produced witnesses to back up their stories. Irynofret had to swear an oath: "If witnesses establish against me that any property of the lady Bakmut was included in the silver I paid for the girl and I have conceded the fact then I shall be liable for 100 [lashes], having also forfeited her."

Our records break off where Bakmut's witnesses substantiate her claim, and the outcome of the proceedings is not known. If Irynofret did lose her case, her punishment would have been severe indeed. Other court cases indicate that women as well as men could be subjected to harsh punishments.

The tomb of Senedjem, located at Deir al-Medina, is the most beautiful of the tombs at this site, and is dated to the Nineteenth Dynasty. The tomb was found in 1886 with funerary furniture inside. The burial chamber in the tomb has a domed ceiling, and beautiful scenes are painted on the walls.

The Valley of the Kings

The Valley of the Kings is the most special place in Thebes, with over sixty-three tombs found; only twenty-six of them belonging kings. Each tomb is different from the others because it is essentially the vision of each king for his afterlife. Most of the tombs contain scenes of the king in front of gods and goddesses, as well as scenes from the religious books, including the "Book of Gates," the "Book of What is in the Underworld" (known as the Imy-duat), the "Book of Re," the "Book of Caverns," and the "Book of the Dead."

The first great discovery in the Valley of the Kings occurred in 1905, seventeen years before the discovery of the tomb of Tutankhamon. This was the tomb of Yuya and Thuya, the father and mother of Queen Tiye, wife of Amenhotep III. Inside the tomb were amazing artifacts, such as gilded coffins, a beautifully painted box that bears the names of Amenhotep III and Queen Tiye, the mummies of Yuya and Thuya, and many other wonderful objects.

Before this discovery, Victor Loret, a French archaeologist, located the tomb of Amenhotep II in 1898. A great sarcophagus was found inside the

tomb containing the mummy of the king. The tomb was beautifully decorated with religious scenes from the "Book of What is in the Underworld."
A major feature of the tomb of Amenhotep II is that it was found semi-
intact with papyrus, statues, and other magical objects. The most
important find, however, was the other twelve royal mummies. Howard
Carter moved nine of the identified mummies to the Egyptian Museum in
Cairo in 1903; he left three in the tomb, one known as the "Elder Lady,"
another called the "Younger Lady" that some believe could be Queen
Nefertiti, and one of a young boy.

The official opening of Tutankhamon's tomb took place on November
29, 1922. The tomb consists of a stairway, a descending corridor, and four
chambers. The corridor leads to the antechamber, a rectangular room with
walls that were lined with piles of furniture and boxes. At the north end of
this room, a sealed doorway, flanked by two life-size statues of the king,
blocked the entrance to the burial chamber. When this blockade was
removed, a huge shrine of gilded wood was revealed, the first of a nest of
four such shrines, of decreasing size, which protected the sarcophagus and
three nested coffins. A doorway in the east wall of the burial chamber led
to the treasury, guarded by a life-size figure of the jackal god Anubis on
top of a shrine-shaped box. Inside this chamber were wooden shrines,
painted black, containing statues of gods, goddesses, and the king in ritual
poses, several boats, and boxes, some filled with jewelry. The fourth room
opened onto the west wall of the antechamber; this was filled with a jum-
ble of miscellaneous objects. It took Carter and his team of English and
American experts about a decade to clear the tomb, conserving and restor-
ing each object and packing it carefully for transport to the Egyptian
Museum in Cairo.

Tutankhamon died at about the age of 19 of what was for years believed
to be a murderous blow to the back of the head. His mummy in fact shows
no such injury, but a break just above his left knee (also noted by Carter's
team), which could have become infected, was the likely cause of death.

Evidence surrounding Tutankhamon's family is inconclusive. He was
most likely the son of Akhenaten and a minor wife, perhaps Kiya. In

January of 1907, Edward Ayrton discovered another tomb in the Valley of the Kings: KV 55. Beyond the entrance lay a corridor, partially filled with pieces of limestone, which led into a rectangular burial chamber containing a gilded and inlaid wooden coffin. Inside this coffin rested a badly decayed mummy, which had been reduced to little more than a skeleton. The lower three-quarters of the coffin's gilded mask had been ripped away and the cartouches (oval rings containing royal names) that once identified the owner were removed, leaving the remains inside both faceless and nameless. The royal coffin and the mummy have only recently been identified as Akhenaten's.

The tomb of Seti I, son of Ramesses I, was found by Giovanni Belzoni in 1817. It is one of the largest tombs in the Valley, and could well be the first fully decorated tomb, as well as one of the most beautiful. Scenes from religious books appear for the first time, such as the "Litany of Re," as well as scenes from the "Book of What is in the Underworld." Belzoni also found the calcite sarcophagus of Seti I, which is now in the Soane Museum in London. His mummy, however, was found in the Deir al-Bahari cache of mummies that was discovered in 1881.

Karnak: the First Pylon and the ram-headed sphinxes

Karnak: the Great Hypostyle Hall

Karnak: the Sacred Lake

Aerial view of the
Karnak Temple complex

Karnak: the First Pylon of the Temple of Amon

Karnak: ram-headed
sphinxes in the Great Court
of the Temple of Amon

Karnak: the Hypostyle Hall of the Temple of Amon

Karnak: the Great Court of the Temple of Amon (opposite)

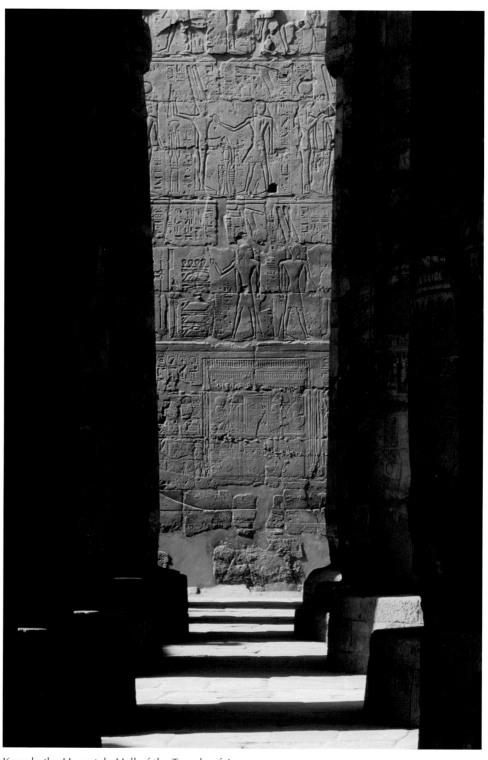

Karnak: the Hypostyle Hall of the Temple of Amon

Karnak: the Hypostyle Hall of the Temple of Amon

Karnak: statue of Thutmosis III in the Temple of Amon

Karnak: statues in the
Hypostyle Hall of the
Temple of Amon (oppos

Karnak: Seti I with the goddess Isis, on the wall
of the Hypostyle Hall of the Temple of Amon

Karnak: entrance to the
Temple of Ramesses II

Karnak: obelisks of Thutmosis I (left) and Hatshepsut, Temple of Amon

Karnak: the Sacred Lake, with the First Pylon and the Hypostyle Hall, Temple of Amon

Karnak: the Sacred Lake, with the Eighth Pylon, Temple of Amon

Luxor Temple and the Avenue of Sphinxes

Luxor Temple, the Great Colonnade

The Colossi of
Memnon at dawn

The Temple of Hatshepsut, Deir al-Bahari

The Ramesseum
(Temple of Ramesses II)

Colossal head of Ramesses II
in the Ramesseum

Hall of Columns at the Ramesseum

Tombs on the Theban West Bank

Mourning scene in the tomb of Ramose, Tombs of the Nobles

Scene from the tomb of Ramose, Tombs of the Nobles

cenes of daily life in the New Kingdom, from the Tombs of the Nobles

The workers' village of Deir al-Medina

The Valley of the Kings

The anthropoid sarcophagus of Ramesses VI, Valley of the Kings

The burial chamber of Ramesses VI, Valley of the Kings

The burial chamber of Ramesses IV, Valley of the Kings

The astronomical ceiling in the tomb of Seti I, Valley of the Kings

The god Horus in the tomb of
Nefertari, Valley of the Queen

The Karnak Temple
Sound and Light Show

Stage 1

May the evening soothe and welcome you, o travelers from Upper Egypt.

You will travel no further because you are come. Here, you are at the beginning of time.

Here was conceived, and lived, the Great Week of the Creation of the World and the Separation of the Earth from the Waters. You are at the House of the Father.

In this House of the Father each Pharaoh thought of himself as a son, and wished to leave his mark upon it.

Each added, superimposed, overdid, outdid through a span of twenty centuries.

The result is this fabulous labyrinth of façades and passages, esplanades and corridors, perspectives and detours to which only priests and Pharaoh had access.

Stage 2

The solemn threshold you have just crossed was forbidden to common mortals.

The City of God was a fortress where a whole garrison of mystic votaries watched over the great Divine Scheme of Things: sunrises, eclipses of the moon, dynastic chains, the bark of night, the bounds of immortality.

The Father is like unto an aged shepherd. His right hand holds the shepherd's crook that gathers in the dust of the stars. His left hand fondles a wild ram walking with him. He is the God of the First Day. It is He who is called Amon.

At the very mention of His Name priests bow the head, and mere mortals prostrate themselves in the dust. Sometimes Ram and God blend together, and a curly browed sphinx can be seen leading the flock, like this one that the sculptor has fashioned in multiplicity to guard the Court of Karnak.

In the time of its full splendor, this citadel could only be reached by a Royal Canal and a Sacred Avenue. The Pharaoh, aboard his Barge of Glory, could moor here, welcomed on the Holy Quayside in the shade of the sycamores by the Pontiff and his numberless retinue of priests with their feather fans.

Do not be overwhelmed by the sheer size of these ruins.

The citadel that arose here was not designed on the scale of men, but on the grand scale of God, from whom all things flowed: the drought and the flood, the granaries and the plagues, dreams and power, death and survival.

And if one of you this evening were to voice the question that you are whispering in your hearts: 'Who art Thou, Amon?' The answer would seep from these walls, these lintels, these pedestals, these secret chambers, these piled ruins ... for the answer is written everywhere in a thousand different hieroglyphics.

I am the Father of Fathers, the Mother of Mothers, and the bull of the seven Celestial Kine.

I opened my mouth to speak in the midst of silence.

I caused to be that men should have a path on which to tread.

I opened the eyes of all that they might see.

My right eye is the day.

My left eye is the night.

And the waters of the Nile spurt from my sandals.

Amon, the Father of all things, had for wife the Goddess Mut, who sat a little below him, wearing her royal headdress of vulture feathers. Near to the Father and the Mother is the Son, Khons, standing rigid as a mummy with a crescent moon picked out upon his oblong head. They made up the Karnak Triad, the Holy Family for whom, and for two thousand years, ceaselessly, complex fortifications were built by the hands of men.

Here, in this place, I, Seti, built the resting place for the Holy Barques beside the avenue. It is made up of three contiguous sandstone chapels. The Chapel of Amon's Barque is in the center, the chapel of Khons is to the east, the Chapel of Mut to the west. I believe this edifice is worthy of Amon and worthy long to bear witness to the glory of Seti II.

I, Ramesses III, conceived that more than one resting place was needed for the Sacred Barques of the Holy Family. So, midway between the sanctuary and the river, I brought into being this edifice ... a veritable temple with pylon guarded by colossi, peristyle courtyard, pillared hall, and sanctuary.

I, Tutankhamon, the youthful Pharaoh who re-established Amon in all his power and glory after the treachery of my brother, I have left behind me in this courtyard nothing but this calcite sphinx.

I, Taharqa, a Nubian reigning late in a crumbling dynasty, built this central pavilion of which little now remains but a specimen of the papyrus-capped gracious colonnade, and an alabaster block that served as an altar for the Divine Ark.

I, a Pharaoh whose name is lost ... so many contradictions are graven on my pedestal ... I left the symbolic image of all the Pharaohs, this gigantic statue rising against the western side of the second pylon, clasping to its legs the tiny figure of a beloved queen.

And I, Ramesses II, the grand elder of the Ramessid Dynasty, the Flame of the Nineteenth Dynasty, I claim the honor, more than three thousand years ago, of having completed this second pylon you are about to pass. At its foot I placed the stele telling of the victory of Kamoses over the Hyksos from the east. Two of my images watched over the gate of the sanctuary. Only the southern statue has remained intact, but it is enough to keep alive the memory of my august reign. For sixty-seven years I wore the double crown of Upper and Lower Egypt. Three royal queens shared my bed. The third was the daughter of the Hittite King, the most powerful monarch of Asia Minor. You may measure the vastness of my Empire, but to judge the span of my life, know that after her I married four of my own daughters, and that the number of my children was ninety-two boys and one-hundred-and-six girls.

I, a Pharaoh of the later period, a king of the twilight, Ptolemy Euergetes II ... I built this marvelous gate leading to the Chambers of God. The panels are of genuine cedar of the Lebanon, lined with Asian copper. May they open to you this evening, and give you access to the most secret, most impressive part of the Karnak labyrinth.

STAGE 3

Lofty and mysterious as a petrified oasis, this is the dwelling of Amon.

These are the mighty stone organ pipes of Karnak.

Let's listen a while to the confused hubbub of words that seem to seep from these walls, thick with the inscriptions of signatures and prayers. Let's dream in this forest of symbols.

The columns are all inspired by the umbelliferous papyrus of the river, which brought to Egypt both its grace and its knowledge. Some of the columns are open—that is to say their *capitals* are open; while others are closed, like the flowers in the bud. The Hypostyle Chamber was built by Seti I between the second and third pylons, and he decorated a large part of the walls and the columns with reliefs. The decoration was completed by Ramesses II who used, not reliefs this time, but sunken reliefs. This hypostyle chamber is the mother of all the three nave basilicas which later were inspired by his plans.

The function of this chamber is essentially both religious and imperial. The physical presence of Amon was there in the form of a statue transported on a barque. And Pharaoh came here to regenerate his soul, since he reigned over Upper and Lower Egypt, in other words over the universe, in his quality as Son of Amon.

Let's admire this cluster of columns in which the architect has striven to capture the very sap of the Nile in the stone, that sap that feeds the giant papyrus clumps springing from the rich silt, swarming with birds and reptiles: the Nile, so like the Egyptian language, with its poetic vitality flowering even beyond the boundaries of death.

It is dawn, and we can imagine the daily awakening of Egypt, as if her hieroglyphics were suddenly to shake themselves from slumber.

In the depths of the sanctuary, Amon the God, the Creator, is present in the form of his statue. There is the ceremonial for the opening of his mouth, for the mouth orders both men and events. There are polishings, fumigations, repeated annointings, touchings of the face with a fork of silex, and an adze, blessing the hoof of an ox—all these solemn rites have literally incorporated the soul of Amon in its receptacle of sculptured wood.

Pharaoh came into the Divine Presence this morning. He purified himself in the waters of the Sacred Lake. He will proceed to awaken the God with his retinue of priests, for the God is still sleeping, as every night, in his tabernacle that is sealed every evening.

Awake Karnak, Queen of the dwellings of the Gods and Goddesses that inhabit her. Awake Gods and Goddesses to the beauty of this new day! Awake in peace, Amon, Lord of Karnak.

The bond is broken, the seal unsealed. The twin gates of Heaven are opening. The twin gates of the Earth are swinging wide.

Hail to Thee, Amon, Lord of Thebes, Lord of Lords, Master of Terror and King of Calm.

The Pharaoh's incantations are done. The ceremony will continue all day long around the awakened statue with the assistance of a host of priests.

God will be nourished with incense and libations. The remains of the offerings of meat and wine will naturally serve to feed the priests. After the noon libations, God will be entertained with paints, oils, perfumes, and jewels.

And in the evening, after a further purification, the statue will return to its tabernacle, sheltered behind a fresh clay seal applied to the gates.

Now God is resting, we must leave the sanctuary. The sun has vanished behind the Theban mountains. Amon has vanished into the night with the sun, embarking once more upon that dark voyage that is the foretaste of death.

Stage 4

This Sacred Lake, on the banks of which you have come to dream—for one can only understand by dreaming—this mirror set in the rock, has reflected the finest firework display of antiquity.

The dazzling gleam that has lasted twenty centuries. As soon as one cluster of stars faded, another Pharaoh fired another salvo. And this will be named forever the splendor of Thebes.

It has been said that Thebes was the first city, the city of cities. Homer named it the City of a Hundred Gates, for a hundred trumpets sounded its fame.

Listen to the sounds of Karnak. The silence was deceptive, since the city, for twenty centuries, has resounded so much to the sound of song and harp that it was almost alive with music.

Naturally there are the baser tasks of the city, the crowded farmyards, the laden trellises, the papyrus presses, and the nobler tasks, the working of gold and silver, the polishing of the columns, the fashioning of the sandstone blocks.

But above all there is the fabulous machinery of the universe, for God is in charge, and is responsible for the functioning of the world.

Upon the terraces priest astronomers observe the movement of the stars, are responsible for eclipses of the moon and the rising of the sun.

Other wise men, bending over their desks, keep the maps of the Empire up to date, and the much more complicated maps of the Kingdom of Eternity.

Watching over the furnaces, others supervised the mysterious metallurgical union of the silver and gold into electrum whose shining plaques would clothe the obelisks.

Look now, over the river to the west bank where the sun sets every evening behind the Valley of the Kings.

It is the shore of the dead … The beginning of the Beyond.

If some lights are still shining in the Necropolis, it means that the embalmers are late at their work.

Their patron is Anubis, the somber God who prowls like a black dog around the cemeteries. Their God is Osiris who knows all the secrets of the resurrection and watches seventy nights over the mummification workshops and the endless swathes of wrappings.

We are at the turning point of the Eighteenth and Nineteenth Dynasties, more than three thousand years ago. Before it, every Thuthmosis and Amenophis, after it, every Seti and Ramesses. Now we are at the moment of unbelievable sacrilege and revolution.

   Amenophis IV changes his name, his God and his capital.

Above all glories he set love supreme. And his beloved wife Nefertiti shared his dream of a new faith and a new city.

Amon no longer existed. Even his name was effaced from the monuments. The new God was called Aton.

The heretical Pharaoh took the name of Akhenaton, devoting himself to his new worship, his poems, his prophecies, his new city of al-Amarna.

And Karnak seemed to be relegated to the shadows …

But the new religion lasted only as long as its inventor. The chisel, ruin, and fire all conspired to obliterate his image.

The new Pharaoh was a child.

This child was to restore the ancient worship.

He rekindled the thousand lamps of the abandoned temples of Karnak. He took the traditional name, and if his earthly life was short, since he died in his adolescence, his posthumous glory eclipses that of all the others ... for his name is Tuthankhamon.

His makeshift tomb was dug in the very floor of the Valley of the Kings ... over there.

It escaped the looters for three thousand years. And in 1922 everything was there.

The sarcophagi, one inside the other, the statues, the jewels of gold, the sacred and profane furniture, the alabasters, the porcelains, that prodigious treasure that still draws the crowds, and that mask encrusted with lapis-lazuli and cornelian which stares at us from the depths of the night with the enigmatic smile of an immortal young man.

Let us return for a moment to the distant centuries when the world's first great queen, Hatshepsut, was inspired to dedicate two golden obelisks to Amon. Listen ...

Behold, I was sitting in my palace, meditating upon the Being who created me, when the voice of my heart spoke, telling me to make two golden obelisks for Him. My spirit took fire thinking of what the men who would later see these monuments would say. They would say, 'Why this mountain of gold?'

But my dream was beyond my power. My two obelisks were not of gold, but a single stone, hard granite without a join, and the expedition to bring the stone to me took seven months.

Now the two obelisks have been set up, I must finish their dedication. I shall add this: 'Thinking of future men who will not have seen the realization of my dream of gold, I wish at least that they may be able to say this ... That my mouth was excellent in the words that issued from it, and that even in granite I never went back on my word.'

Torn from their native land, today obelisks rise in all the capitals of the modern world ... in Rome, Paris, London, Istanbul, New York.

Above the vain tumult of cities these stones stand like fingers raised for silence, preserving the tradition of ancient Egypt's meditation.

And the breath of Amon turns the machinery of the world in the heart of the forbidden city.

But each year, the harvest done, the grapes gathered, when the new wine rises to the head, Amon takes a short holiday. On his Barge of State he sets forth for a honeymoon on the river.

He goes to Luxor where he honeymoons each year with the Goddess Amonet.

This is the Beautiful Festival of Opet. The joyous echoes still seem to come down to us from the depths of time. All the details are inscribed on the walls along the great Colonnade at Luxor.

Once again, in this month of Paophi, the people of Thebes are gathering at the gates of Karnak for the grand festival of the God Amon.

It is enough to hear the laughter to know that the granaries are full and that the grapes are already fermented.

Silence. Here come the standards and banners that open the procession.

The barque porters are moving off again from their resting point.
There's the Ram's Head, at the prow of the Divine Barque.

The Barques of Mut, Khons and the Pharaoh are following in order … and
you can just make out the baskets of fruit and flowers through the plumed
parasols.

The front of procession has reached the landing stage.
   Amon is hoisted on his vessel, and it swings to face the current.

But the current is strong, and the bare-chested men in the towing tugs row
for all they're worth.

And they never succeed if the men on the banks were not holding on the
cables.

Listen to the daraboukka players, rhythming the oarsmen.

Look … The mist is clearing.

One behind the other you can see the Divine Barques ... as dazzling as the
sun.

The Sacred Fleet has reached Luxor.
   Luxor, that the people call 'The Harem of God.'

And how could it be better expressed? This tender mystery that will reign
over Luxor for ten days and ten nights so that the world may be reborn,
that the cattle may multiply, and the earth be fertile.

Take Thy joy, o Amon …

… and give us joy too during these days of feast …

... while we await Thy return on the eleventh day and Thy glorious descent of the Nile ...

... and Thy return to Karnak.

Yet the twilight fell over the City of God as it falls over all things.

The boots of the great conquerors rang on the paving stones of antiquity.

Assurbanipal the Assyrian reached the gates of Thebes and defied the ancient citadel.

Alexander of Macedon wished to add the title of Pharaoh to his glories.

Caesar the Roman clutched all the Mediterranean in his eager hand, and opened it only to give a last caress to conquered Egypt.

Like a tree that has grown too old, Amon himself knew no return of spring.

But the line of Aton, born of the dream of a Pharaoh who was a poet, was luckier than the Patriarch of Karnak. It was the 'one God' of Akhenaton, the 'Our Father' of the Christians and the Muslims who raised chapels and mosques in the dust of Thebes.

But though the testimonies of a faith may fall into ruins, they do not die. A language may be lost, but it will be found.

And Amon, who reigns forever here, is not a God to be taken lightly.

He is a God of the Beginning when the earth and the waters were still mingled as were the animals and men. He is a complex God as powerful as the Creation.

Amon announced the salvation of man.

He also announced the salvation of the crocodile and the scarab, everything that moves of the flowers of the earth. He deigned to assume the
guise of a ram, a falcon, a goose, or a bull. He offered equality to all the
companions of the universe.

And the language of the hieroglyphics is like this overwhelming faith,
which thanks to the floods of the Nile, raised these pylons, these colonnades, these obelisks.

May these hieroglyphics come to life once more to bid farewell to you,
new pilgrims to Upper Egypt, like a sudden flight of a myriad sacred birds,
their spread wings sprinkling the droplets of the river like a benediction.

Suggestions for Further Reading

The British Museum Book of Ancient Egypt, edited by A. J. Spencer.
British Museum Press, The American University in Cairo Press, 2007.

The Complete Gods and Goddesses of Ancient Egypt, Richard H.
Wilkinson. Thames & Hudson, The American University in Cairo
Press, 2005.

*The Complete Valley of the Kings: Tombs and Treasures of Egypt's
Greatest Pharaohs,* Nicholas Reeves and Richard H. Wilkinson.
Thames & Hudson, The American University in Cairo Press, 2002.

The Golden King: The World of Tutankhamun, Zahi Hawass. National
Geographic, The American University in Cairo Press, 2006.

A History of Egypt: From Earliest Times to the Present, Jason
Thompson. Haus Publishing, The American University in Cairo Press,
2008.